I Have A Mayor Named Keisha!

Brown Girl Resilience Books
Keisha Lance Bottoms, Atlanta's 60th Mayor

Coloring Book

Charell G. Coleman
Cover art by Kayla Holloway
Illustration by Zuri Book Pros

ISBN: 979-8-9862589-7-3

∞ This paper meets the requirements of ANSI/NISO Z39.48-1992 (Permanence of Paper)

Cover Art by Kayla Holloway
Illustrations by zuribookpros.com

072622

Brown Girl Resilience

The Brown Girl Resilience books pays homage to people of color, our ancestors, and the practice of resilience. Resilience deals with the challenges that life presents while acknowledging the harm it has caused in our past and how it has forever changed our physical and emotional beings. As we move through and past our hurt, this refinement process creates a more polished version of us. Sharing our stories, having the courage to put our masks away, unveiling who we are at our core, and acknowledging that we are indeed scarred, yet transforming and healing, gives us the validation we deserve in this world.

While society magnifies these scars through some forms of media, entertainment, and various organized systems, people of color have used these occurrences as resilience tools. These tools help identify the origins of our adversities and roots of trauma, focus on things within our control, and help us respond using therapeutic wellness skills and healthy approaches. These stories offer hope of creating a world of peace and equality for all humanity. With these stories, may our minds and souls create conscious narratives that acknowledge where we are presently and continue for generations as we learn to "just be human"!

FREDERICK DOUGLASS
HIGH.

ATLANTA GOT A MAYOR NAM
Keisha
..... and she's a Delta.

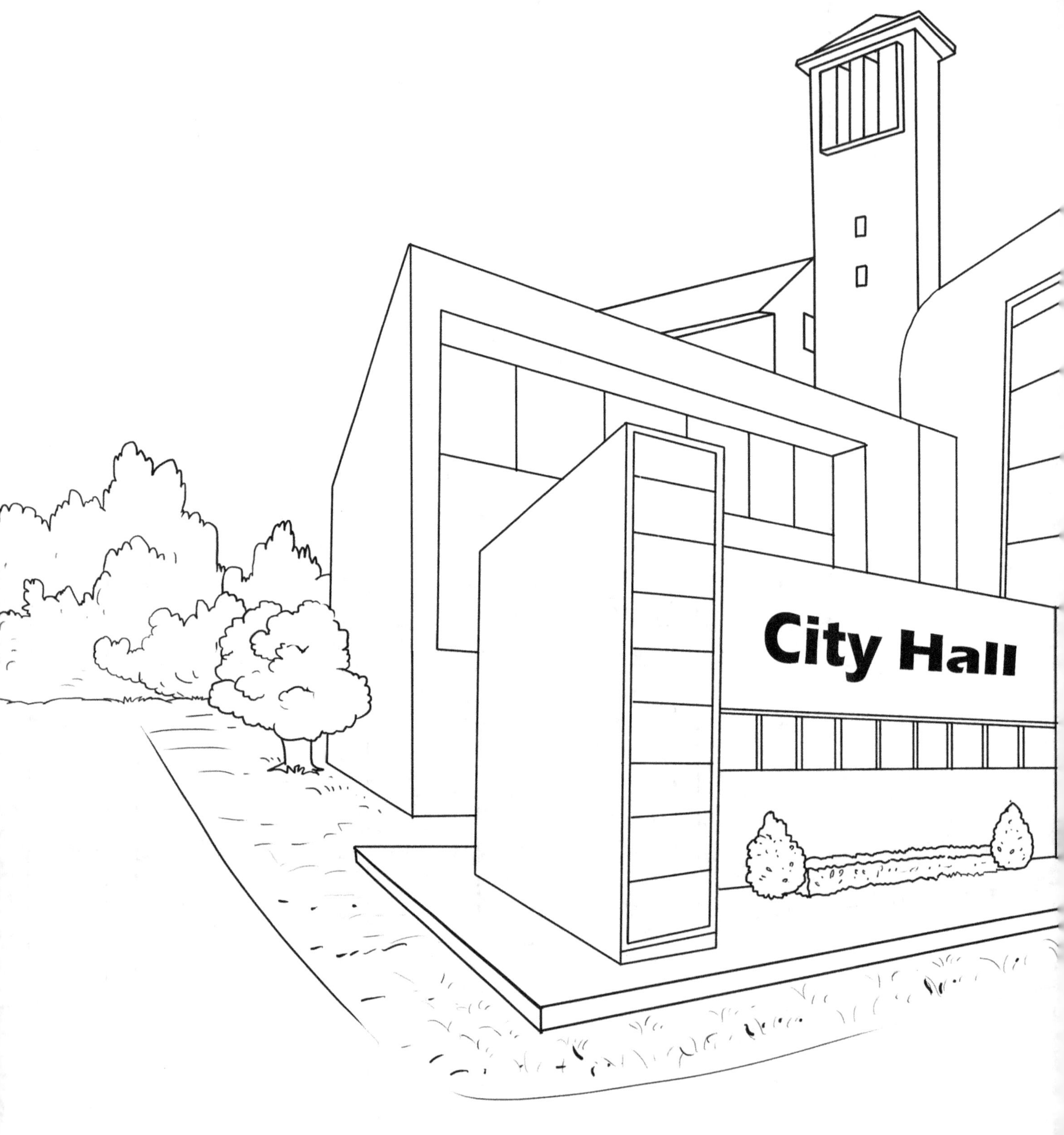
City Hall

14

KEISHA
LANCE BOTTOMS

For
Mayor

KEISHA

Keisha

Lance Bottoms

IMMIGRATION CHAOS
ATLANTA MAYOR ORDERS CITY JAIL TO
Mayor Keisha Lance Bottoms

REJECT NEW ICE DETAINEES

Housing
Trust Fund

26

I CAN'T BREATHE
ONE
Atlanta

BIDEN
PRESIDENT

A Note to Mom

My mom is a great mayor because she always makes sure the city is first and that Atlanta is perfectly ready for anyone who visits our city. She is a great mom and always makes time to be with us, no matter how busy she gets. She does things for our family and still handles the business for our city. That's why I love my mom so much.

—Langston Bottoms

It feels amazing for my mom to run the city because it helps me to know that women can do anything, especially black girl magic. She inspires me. Because of her, I know that if you put in the work you can become anything, even a star!

—Lincoln and Lennox Bottoms
(Mayor Bottoms' twin daughter and son.)